CREATE with
DUCT
TAPE

# DUCT TAPE
## Survival Gear

by Rebecca Felix

Lerner Publications ◆ Minneapolis

Lerner Publications Company
A division of Lerner Publishing Group, Inc.
241 First Avenue North
Minneapolis, MN 55401 USA

For reading levels and more information, look up this title at www.lernerbooks.com.

Main body text set in Bembo. Typeface provided by Monotype.

**Library of Congress Cataloging-in-Publication Data**

The Cataloging-in-Publication Data for Duct Tape Survival Gear is on file at the Library of Congress.
ISBN 978-1-5124-2666-3 (lib. bdg.)
ISBN 978-1-5124-2763-9 (EB pdf)

LC record available at https://lccn.loc.gov/2016017122

Manufactured in the United States of America
1-41432-23337-8/10/2016

# Contents

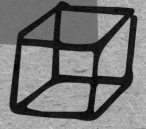

# World's Toughest Tape

What can patch a spacecraft but tear to pieces with your fingers? What is superstrong and **waterproof**? It's extra sticky and has all kinds of uses. It's duct tape!

This sticky stuff was first known as *duck tape*. The tape got its name because it was fantastic at **repelling** water, just like a duck's feathers. During World War II (1939–1945), soldiers used the tape to repair military vehicles. Word spread about this terrific tape. Soon it was stocked in hardware stores and homes across the United States.

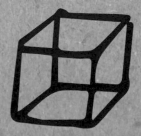

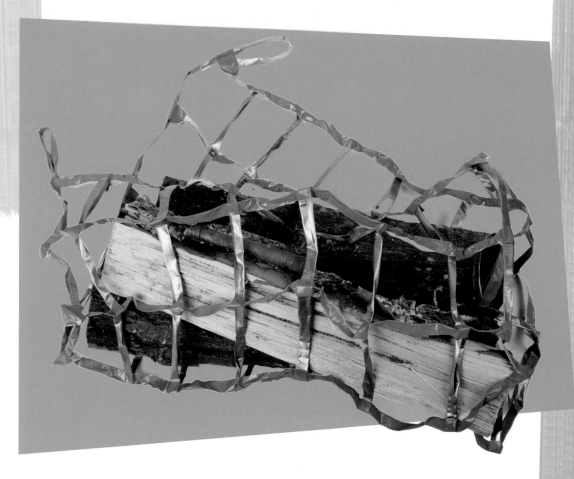

People began using duck tape for tons of tasks. One important duck-tape job was connecting **air ducts**. The tape was just as strong as the screws and bolts usually used to hold air ducts together. Binding these big, silver tubes became such a common use that the tape was renamed duct tape.

Did you know duct tape has also been used to make survival gear? People have made tents, tarps, stretchers, and even splints and casts out of the supersticky tape. What if you were stranded in the wilderness with just a roll of duct tape? What items could you craft to help you survive? Turn the page and find out how to rip, stick, and attach your very own duct tape survival gear.

# Before You
# Get Started

## Sticky Supply

Part of what makes duct tape such a super supply is how sticky it is. But this can also make crafting with duct tape tricky. Every strip counts! Work slowly and carefully to avoid accidentally getting pieces stuck together. Be aware that duct tape may be hard to remove from certain surfaces. It may also leave a sticky **residue** behind.

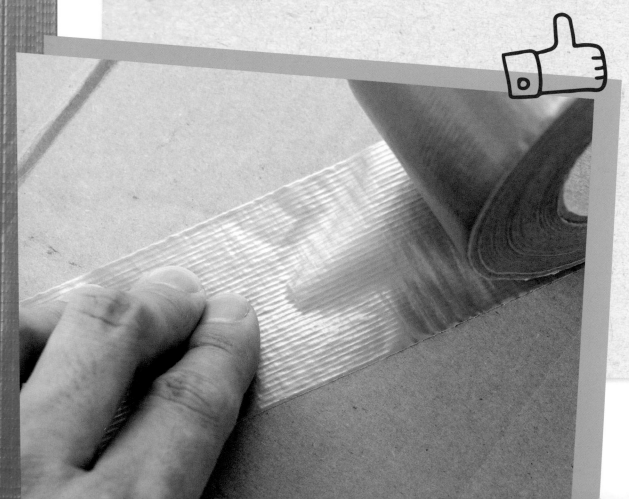

# Wilderness Workspace

A clean workspace is important any time you craft and construct. This is also true when you're working in the wilderness! If the sticky side of a duct tape strip gets covered with dirt, leaves, or grass, it may become unusable. Clear a workspace before creating your survival gear. Be sure you remove loose leaves, grass, dirt, and other **debris**.

## Super Strength

What makes duct tape so strong? The secret is in its design. Duct tape has fibers woven in a crisscross pattern. These fibers keep the tape intact even under lots of pressure.

# Dynamic Duct Tape

Of course, duct tape is useful. But what makes it really amazing is your imagination! As you create survival gear from this sticky tape, think about what other things you could create. In a pinch, small strips of duct tape could be used to fix broken tools or mend holes in clothing and shoes. If you had enough rolls, you could even make a duct tape tent. Dream big and get creative!

# Stay Safe!

Check with an adult before you start any new duct tape project. Never stick duct tape on your or someone else's face or over eyes, ears, or mouths. Do not place duct tape on an open wound. Never bind a body part with duct tape. Ask for an adult's help when using sharp objects, such as scissors. Be smart and safe as you create some terrific duct tape projects!

# Nifty Net

Craft a neat net to help carry your survival supplies.

## Sticky Tip

Remember that duct tape can leave residue behind. Make sure you ask an adult before you stick tape to a table, counter, or other surface.

## Materials
• duct tape

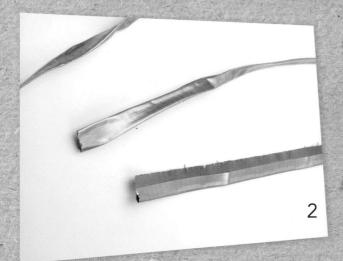

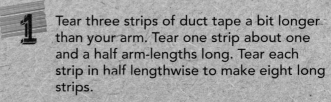

**1** Tear three strips of duct tape a bit longer than your arm. Tear one strip about one and a half arm-lengths long. Tear each strip in half lengthwise to make eight long strips.

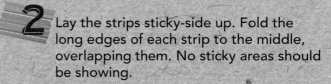

**2** Lay the strips sticky-side up. Fold the long edges of each strip to the middle, overlapping them. No sticky areas should be showing.

2

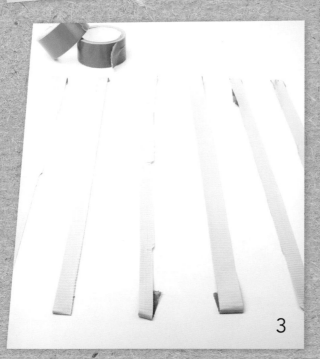

**3** Tear four more strips of duct tape about the length of your arm. Tear each strip in half lengthwise to make eight long strips. Arrange these strips in rows, sticky-side up. Fold the ends of each strip under to hold the tape in place.

**4** Arrange the strips you made in steps 1 and 2 in a grid across the rows you made in step 3. Place the two longest strips at the ends. Fold the ends of the long strips at each corner to make loops.

**5** Fold the ends of the strips in the bottom layer over the top layer. Press the sticky sides together.

3

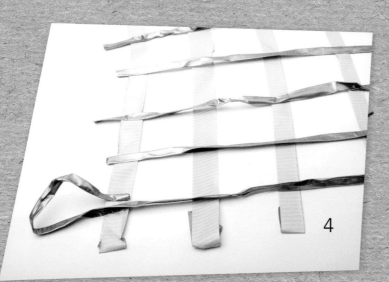

**6** Fold each of the strips in the bottom layer in half lengthwise. Pinch the tape around the strips in the top layer as you get to them. This holds the strips in both layers together. Make sure no sticky areas are showing. Your net is ready for its big adventure!

4

# Superstrong
# Survival Rope

Twist, braid, and knot duct tape strips to create a rope tough enough to handle tons of tasks!

## Materials

- duct tape

## Sticky Tip

To braid the rope, lay the three strips side by side. Cross the left strip over the middle strip. Then cross the right strip over the middle strip.

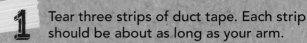

**1** Tear three strips of duct tape. Each strip should be about as long as your arm.

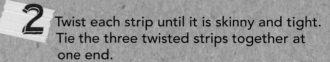

**2** Twist each strip until it is skinny and tight. Tie the three twisted strips together at one end.

**3** Tear additional strips of tape. Tape each new strip to the end of one twisted strip. Then twist each new strip.

**4** Repeat step 3 until the rope is the length you want. Remember, your rope will shorten as you braid it.

**5** Now braid the three strips together. Tie the end in a knot. Your rope is ready to secure your gear!

## Did You Know?

In 1970, NASA astronauts used duct tape to repair a spacecraft while it was in orbit around Earth!

# Crushable Cup

Craft a clever cup for hydrating on the go. When you're done drinking, crush the cup and store it in a pocket.

## Materials
- duct tape

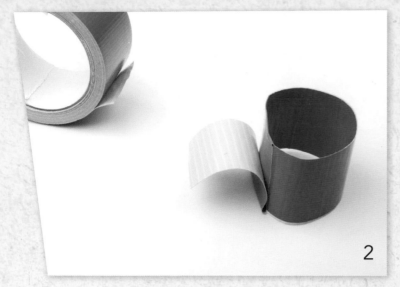

 Tear off two strips of duct tape, each about as long as your **forearm**. Press the sticky sides of the strips together. This makes one strip. Make sure no sticky surfaces are exposed.

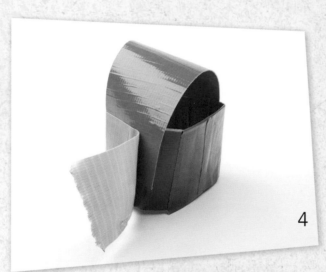

2

 Form the strip into a ring. Wrap another short strip of duct tape around the ring's seam to secure it. This ring makes up the cup's sides.

 Tear off two strips of duct tape, each about as long as your hand. Press the sticky sides of the strips together.

4

 Tape one end to one side of your cup. Tape the other end to the opposite side. The center of the strip should arc over the ring. This is the cup's bottom.

 Repeat steps 3 and 4 to add another strip. Crisscross this strip over the first strip, to make an X over the cup's bottom. Keep repeating steps 3 and 4. Work around the cup until you have created a curved cup bottom with no holes.

5

 Use small strips of duct tape to cover all the seams. This keeps your cup from leaking. Then use your survival cup next time you need a drink!

15

# Wearable
# Water Bottle Holder

Build a go-anywhere water bottle holder for your next adventure!

## Materials
- duct tape
- water bottle

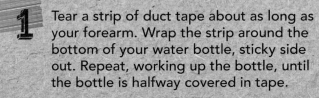

**1** Tear a strip of duct tape about as long as your forearm. Wrap the strip around the bottom of your water bottle, sticky side out. Repeat, working up the bottle, until the bottle is halfway covered in tape.

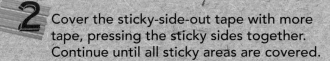

**2** Cover the sticky-side-out tape with more tape, pressing the sticky sides together. Continue until all sticky areas are covered.

1

**3** Tear a strip of duct tape that is a bit longer than you are tall. This will be your strap. Lay this strip flat on the ground, sticky side up. Set the bottle in the center of the strip, so the bottom sticks to the tape.

3

**4** Pull one tape end up, pressing it along the side of the bottle. Stop when you reach the end of the tape, leaving a tail. Tear a strip of tape about as long as the tail. Cover the tail with this strip, pressing the sticky sides together.

**5** Repeat step 4 with the other end of the strap.

**6** Use a short strip of tape to connect the ends of the strap. Now just hang your water bottle holder across your body. Your handy holder is ready for action!

5

# Instant
# Ice Pack

Rip, stick, and fold a waterproof pouch
that makes a perfect ice pack in a pinch.

## Materials
- duct tape
- ice cubes

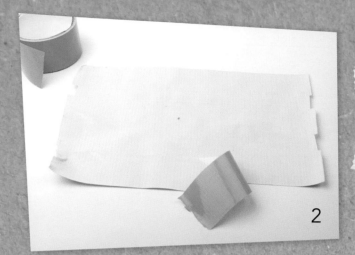

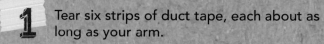

**1** Tear six strips of duct tape, each about as long as your arm.

**2** Overlap the long edge of one strip slightly with the long edge of another strip. Keep them sticky-side up. Repeat with the remaining strips until you've formed a rectangle.

2

**3** Create a second rectangle the exact same size. Carefully lay one rectangle on top of the other, pressing the sticky sides together.

5

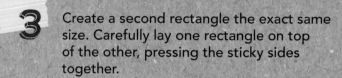

**4** Lay the rectangle down so a short edge is at the bottom. Fold up the bottom edge to make a pouch. Stop when the edge is about three-fourths of the way up the rectangle.

**5** Seal the pouch sides with small strips of duct tape. Make sure the corners are sealed tightly so they don't leak.

6

**6** Tear three small strips of duct tape. Roll each one into a ring with the sticky side out. Place these rings along the top edge of the rectangle. Once you fill your pouch with ice, press the flap closed. Your ice pack is ready for its big chill!

# Easy First-Aid Roll

Craft a carrier for all your first-aid gear!

### Materials

- duct tape
- scissors
- first-aid items, such as bandages, gauze, tweezers, and more

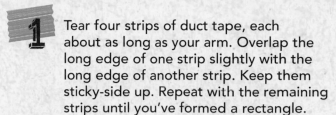

**1** Tear four strips of duct tape, each about as long as your arm. Overlap the long edge of one strip slightly with the long edge of another strip. Keep them sticky-side up. Repeat with the remaining strips until you've formed a rectangle.

**2** Create a second rectangle the exact same size. Carefully lay one rectangle on top of the other, pressing the sticky sides together.

3

**3** Tear two strips of duct tape that are longer than the rectangle. Overlap the long edges of the strips slightly. Keep them sticky-side up. This will become a long pocket. Center it right below the rectangle.

4

**4** Place a strip of duct tape across the long pocket. Press the sticky sides together. Cut off any excess tape. This will be a small pouch in the pocket. Repeat to make more pouches. Be sure to leave sticky areas exposed between each pouch.

**5** Flip the pocket strip up and press it onto the rectangle. The bottom edges of the pocket and the rectangle should line up. Wrap the excess tape on each side of the pocket around the sides of the rectangle. Seal the bottom of the pocket with more tape.

5

**6** Tear a long strip of duct tape and twist it into a rope. Fill the pouches with first-aid items. Then roll up the kit and tie the rope around it!

# Warm and Cozy
# Mittens

Make a pair of snug duct tape mittens to keep your hands warm and dry on chilly days.

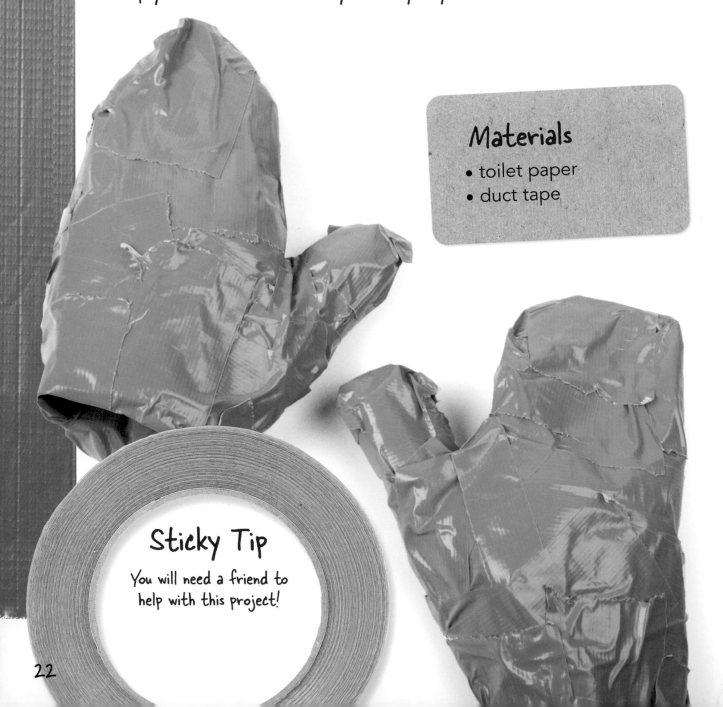

## Materials
- toilet paper
- duct tape

### Sticky Tip

You will need a friend to help with this project!

1

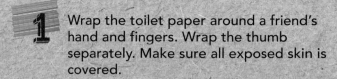

1. Wrap the toilet paper around a friend's hand and fingers. Wrap the thumb separately. Make sure all exposed skin is covered.

2. Completely cover the toilet paper in duct tape. Use many strips of different lengths if needed. Be sure to overlap the tape so the mitten stays together. Don't wrap too tightly! You want to make sure your friend can easily get the mitten on and off.

2

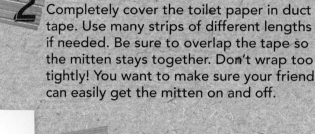

3. Have your friend remove the mitten. Then use short strips of duct tape to cover the edge along the wrist. Make sure no toilet paper sticks out.

4. Repeat steps 1 through 3 using your friend's other hand.

5. Have your friend try out her newly made mittens. Then switch places to have your friend help you make your own mittens!

3

## Survival Safety First!

These mittens are fine for fun. But they should not be used in place of actual gloves or mittens to prevent **frostbite** in the outdoors.

# Rain Shield

Stay dry with this waterproof hood and rain shield!

## Materials

- hooded shirt or jacket
- duct tape
- large plastic trash bag
- scissors

## Sticky Tip

No scissors? Carefully tear head and arm holes in the bag.

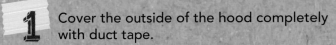
**1** Cover the outside of the hood completely with duct tape.

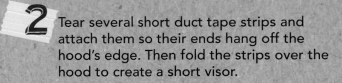
**2** Tear several short duct tape strips and attach them so their ends hang off the hood's edge. Then fold the strips over the hood to create a short visor.

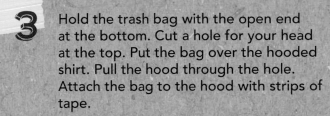
**3** Hold the trash bag with the open end at the bottom. Cut a hole for your head at the top. Put the bag over the hooded shirt. Pull the hood through the hole. Attach the bag to the hood with strips of tape.

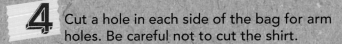
**4** Cut a hole in each side of the bag for arm holes. Be careful not to cut the shirt.

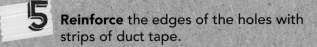
**5** **Reinforce** the edges of the holes with strips of duct tape.

**6** Test out your hooded rain shield on the next rainy day. Patch any holes in the body or hood with additional strips of tape. This will keep you warm and dry!

## Did You Know?

If you used all the duct tape sold in a year, you could make a giant duct tape strip that would stretch to the moon and back.

# Warm Waterproof Boots

Turn any type of shoes into insulated boots that keep warmth in and water out!

## Materials
- old pair of shoes
- 2 plastic trash bags
- duct tape
- 15–20 smaller plastic bags, such as plastic grocery bags

## Sticky Tip
A friend can be helpful when wrapping and taping the boots. Have an assistant handy for this project!

2

 **1** Put on the shoes. If they have laces, tie them loose enough so you can slip your feet in and out.

 **2** Step into one of the trash bags and wrap it around your leg. Secure with a strip of tape.

 **3** Roll the smaller bags up and wrap them around your shoe and leg. The bags will act as insulation. Use tape strips to hold the bags in place.

 **4** Repeat step 3 to add another layer of bags.

*Warm Waterproof Boots continued next page*

3

## Did You Know?

Each summer, the town of Avon, Ohio, holds a duct tape festival.

*Warm Waterproof Boots, continued*

 Wrap the bags around your foot and leg completely in duct tape. Make sure the tape is loose enough for you to slip your foot in and out of the finished boot. Smooth the tape as much as possible while you are wrapping.

 Examine your boot. Cover any places where plastic bags are peeking out. Add a second layer of tape if needed.

 Cover the top edge of the boot. Make sure all plastic bags are covered.

 Repeat steps 2 through 7 to make a second boot.

 Use your duct tape boots to help keep your feet warm and dry as you face the elements!

5

6

7

# Show Off Your
# Survival Skills

Once you've finished some incredible duct tape projects, it's time to test them out! Try using your nifty net to carry supplies, such as firewood. Is it strong enough? Is it big enough? What improvements could you make? Test your duct tape boots on a short hike. But don't forget to bring along a spare roll of duct tape for any on-the-go repairs. And remember, duct tape survival gear is fun, but it isn't a substitute for real gear in the wilderness. If you decide to try hiking in your duct tape boots, be sure to bring along a pair of real hiking boots, just in case.

# Cleanup and Safekeeping

Now you're geared up and ready to go! But don't forget to clean up first. After creating your survival gear, make sure to pick up all your supplies. Collect and discard any duct tape scraps too small to use. But remember, a leftover piece of tape might come in handy later for a repair or new project. If your projects left a sticky residue on any surfaces, be sure to clean it off. Leave your work area cleaner than you found it! Then find a safe place to store your projects where they will stay clean and dry. Make sure they are handy for your next big adventure!

## Keep Creating!

You've seen how duct tape can be used to make supplies on the go. It can also be used to make tons of other tools to help out on wilderness trips! Now that you've made these projects, you're ready to dream up your own duct tape gear. Have fun and keep creating!

# Glossary

**air ducts:** pipes that move air around buildings

**debris:** bits and pieces of objects that are left behind

**forearm:** the part of the arm between the elbow and the wrist

**frostbite:** a condition in which parts of the body are damaged due to extreme cold

**insulated:** to be covered in a material used to stop heat from escaping or entering

**reinforce:** to strengthen something by adding more material

**repelling:** driving off or keeping something away

**residue:** what remains after something else is removed or completed

# Further Information

**15 Uses for Duct Tape at the Campsite**
http://www.reserveamerica.com/outdoors/
15-uses-for-duct-tape-at-the-campsite.htm
Find even more ways you can use duct tape on your next camping trip.

**Formaro, Amanda. *Duct Tape Mania.***
White Plains, NY: Studio Fun International, Inc., 2014.
This project-packed book is full of duct-tape crafts and activities.

**How Duck Tape® Was Named**
http://duckbrand.com/about
Learn the history behind one of the most famous duct tape brands.

**Oxlade, Chris. *Be an Adventurer.***
Minneapolis, MN: Hungry Tomato, 2016.
Learn more survival tricks and trips for your next great adventure!

# Index

Photo Acknowledgments

The images in this book are used with the permission of: © Devonyu/iStockphoto, p. 6; © Feng Yu/Shutterstock Images, pp. 1 (gray tape roll), 4 (gray tape roll), 7 (gray tape roll), 8 (gray tape roll), 10 (gray tape roll), 12 (gray tape roll), 22 (gray tape roll), 24 (gray tape roll), 26 (gray tape roll), 29 (gray tape roll); © Mighty Media, Inc., pp. 1 (gray tape), 1 (orange tape), 2 (green tape), 4 (camo tape), 5 (net craft), 5 (green tape), 5 (yellow tape), 6 (orange tape), 7 (camo tape), 7 (green tape), 8 (ice pack craft), 8 (green tape), 8 (orange tape), 8 (yellow tape), 9 (yellow tape), 10 (orange tape), 10 (net craft), 11 (top), 11 (middle), 11 (bottom), 11 (orange tabs), 12 (rope craft), 12 (blanket), 12 (yellow tape), 13 (top), 13 (middle), 13 (bottom), 13 (yellow tape), 14 (cup craft), 14 (cup with water), 14 (green tape), 15 (top), 15 (middle), 15 (bottom), 15 (green tabs), 16 (water bottle craft), 16 (orange tape), 16 (yellow tape), 17 (top), 17 (middle), 17 (bottom), 17 (orange tabs), 18 (ice pack craft), 18 (yellow tape), 19 (yellow tabs), 19 (top), 19 (middle), 19 (bottom), 20 (first-aid craft), 20 (green tape), 21 (top), 21 (middle), 21 (bottom), 21 (green tabs), 22 (mittens craft), 22 (orange tape), 23 (top), 23 (middle), 23 (bottom), 23 (orange tabs), 23 (yellow tape), 24 (rain shield craft), 24 (yellow tape), 25 (top), 25 (middle), 25 (bottom), 25 (yellow tape), 26 (boots craft), 26 (green tape), 27 (green tape), 27 (top), 27 (bottom), 27 (green tabs), 28 (top), 28 (middle), 28 (bottom), 28 (green tabs), 29 (camo tape), 29 (green tape), 29 (orange tape), 29 (yellow tape), 30 (camo tape), 31 (yellow tape), 32 (green tape), 32 (yellow tape); © mama_mia/Shutterstock Images, pp. 3, 10, 11, 12, 14, 16, 17, 18, 20, 22, 23, 24, 26, 29, 30; © Mckenna_Ringwald/iStockphoto, p. 8; © Monkey Business Images/Shutterstock Images, p. 9; © wongwean/Shutterstock Images, pp. 4 (orange paper), 6 (yellow paper), 13 (orange paper), 15 (yellow paper), 19 (orange paper), 21 (yellow paper), 25 (orange paper), 27 (yellow paper), 28 (yellow paper), 20 (orange paper); © Samuel Borges Photography/Shutterstock Images, p. 29 (boy).

Cover: © Feng Yu/Shutterstock Images (gray tape roll); © Mighty Media, Inc.; © wongwean/Shutterstock Images (orange background).

Back Cover: © Feng Yu/Shutterstock Images (gray tape roll); © wongwean/Shutterstock Images (orange background).